P9-DGW-482

Snorkeling and Diving

Paul Mason

Smart Apple Media

This edition first published in 2008 in the United States of America by Smart Apple Media.
All rights reserved. No part of this book may be reproduced in any form or by any means
without written permission from the publisher.

Smart Apple Media
2140 Howard Drive West
North Mankato, Minnesota 56003

First published in 2007 by
MACMILLAN EDUCATION AUSTRALIA PTY LTD
627 Chapel Street, South Yarra, Australia 3141

Visit our Web site at www.macmillan.com.au or go directly to www.macmillanlibrary.com.au

Associated companies and representatives throughout the world.

Copyright © Paul Mason 2007

Library of Congress Cataloging-in-Publication Data

Mason, Paul, 1967-
    Snorkeling and diving / by Paul Mason.
    p. cm. — (Recreational sports)
    Includes index.
    ISBN 978-1-59920-128-3
    1. Skin diving—Juvenile literature. 2. Scuba diving—Juvenile literature. I. Title.

    GV838.672.M38 2007
    797.2′3—dc22

                                            2007004592

Edited by Vanessa Lanaway
Text and cover design by Pier Vido
Page layout by Pier Vido
Photo research by Naomi Parker
Illustrations by Boris Silvestri
Map on pp. 28–9 by Pier Vido

Printed in U.S.

Acknowledgements
The author and the publisher are grateful to the following for permission to reproduce
copyright material:

Front cover photograph: Snorkeler exploring a reef, courtesy of Stuart Westmorland/Getty
Images.

Photos courtesy of:
Georgette Douwma/Getty Images, p. 24 (top); Stephen Frink/Getty Images, p. 6; Nikolas
Konstantinou/Getty images, p. 19; Darryl Torckler/Getty Images, p. 5; Stuart Westmorland/
Getty Images, pp. 1, 11; David Harasti, p. 30; Pamela Burley/Istockphoto, p. 21; Simon Gurney/
Istockphoto, p. 24 (bottom); Orlando Rosu/Istockphoto, p. 26; Dennis Sabo/Istockphoto, pp.
7, 22; Suzanne Tucker/Istockphoto, p. 10; Matthias Weinrich/Istockphoto, p. 15; Photolibrary,
p. 25; Rosenfeld Alexis/Photolibrary, p. 4; Federico Cabello/Photolibrary, p. 20; Jordan Patricia/
Photolibrary, p. 27; Franklin Viola/Photolibrary, p. 9 (bottom); Photos.com, pp. 8, 9 (top), 12;
Science Photo Library, p. 18.

While every care has been taken to trace and acknowledge copyright, the publisher tenders
their apologies for any accidental infringement where copyright has proved untraceable.
Where the attempt has been unsuccessful, the publisher welcomes information that would
redress the situation.

Please note
At the time of printing, the Internet addresses appearing in this book were correct. However,
because of the dynamic nature of the Internet, we cannot guarantee that all Web addresses
will remain correct.

Contents

Recreational sports   4

Getting started   6

Snorkeling equipment   8

Where to snorkel   10

Getting into the water   12

Saving energy   14

Clearing your snorkel and mask   16

Snorkeling safely   18

Scuba diving   20

Underwater science   22

Fit for the ocean   26

Snorkeling and diving around the world   28

Interview: Underwater crazy!   30

Glossary   31

Index   32

Glossary words

When a word is printed in **bold**, you can look up
its meaning in the glossary on page 31.

Recreational sports

Recreational sports are the activities we do in our spare time. These are sports that people do for fun, not necessarily for competition.

You have probably tried some recreational sports already. Maybe you would like to know more about them or find out about new ones? Try as many as you can—not just snorkeling. Also try biking, hiking, fishing, kayaking, and climbing. This will help you find one you really love doing.

Benefits of sports

Recreational sports give people lots of pleasure, but they also have other benefits. People who exercise regularly usually have better health. They find it easier to concentrate and do better in school or work.

"Even as a kid, I wanted to know how the fish felt."
Tanya Streeter, champion free-diver, explains why she always loved being underwater.

Scuba divers are able to go deeper than snorkelers, to where there is less light and the water is darker.

Snorkeling and diving

Snorkeling and diving take you on a journey to the world below the surface of the sea. There you can see amazing animals and incredible underwater landscapes. Australia's Great Barrier Reef is one of the most popular places in the world for snorkeling and diving, but there are many others.

Snorkeling

Snorkeling is simple, cheap, and easy to learn if you are a good swimmer. All you need to snorkel in warm water is a mask, snorkel, and fins. In colder water, a wet suit helps you keep warm.

WATCH OUT!
Never go snorkeling or diving without a buddy.

Diving

Diving is more complicated and expensive than snorkeling. In most countries you have to be at least 12 years old to learn to dive.

Shallow water is best for snorkeling, because all the best sights are in easy reach.

Getting started

Visiting the underwater world is a bit like flying. You skim above the seabed with no visible support, like a bird swooping through the sky.

What is snorkeling?

Snorkeling is swimming with your face underwater, breathing through a special tube that reaches up into the air. The tube is called a snorkel. Snorkelers dive down to explore below the surface. They stay underwater for as long as they can hold their breath. Then they have to come back to the surface to breathe.

Air sucked in here

Mouth underwater

Breathe in here

A snorkel is a simple tube that lets humans breathe underwater.

Snorkeling is usually most fun in areas where the water is fairly shallow. It is easier to dive down if you spot something interesting on the seabed.

Cost of snorkeling

You can start snorkeling without spending a lot of money. You don't need much equipment, and it is easy to carry around. You can easily load all of your gear into a backpack and head off to the sea.

Divers can explore far below the surface of the sea.

What is diving?

Diving is swimming underwater while carrying a supply of air with you. Divers usually carry their air supply in metal tanks on their back.

Divers do not have to come up to the surface for a breath. Instead, they breathe the air from their tanks. They can stay underwater for a long time—up to an hour. Most people learn to dive by joining a diving club or going on a specialist course.

"I can only think of one experience which might exceed in interest a few hours spent underwater, and that would be a journey to Mars."

William Beebe, American naturalist and undersea explorer.

Snorkeling equipment

Snorkelers do not need much equipment. A mask and snorkel are the basics. Fins, a wet suit, and other equipment can be added later.

Masks

There are lots of different kinds of masks. It is important for your mask to fit your face well. If it is too big, water might get in at the edges. If it is too small, it will be uncomfortable. The right-sized mask will fit comfortably around your eyes, forehead, and nose. Some masks have curved lenses, which give 180-degree vision.

A face mask for snorkeling or diving.

Silicone does not rot in sunlight and seawater

Face-fitting skirt

Straps can be tightened or loosened to fit

Polycarbonate lenses are very tough

Fins

Fins come in many different designs. The most important thing is that they are comfortable. Also, make sure your fins are not too big, or kicking will become tiring.

Snorkels

The simplest snorkel is just a straight tube with a curve at the bottom. At the curved end is a mouthpiece. The straight end sticks out of the water into the air, and lets you breathe. Some snorkels are designed to stop water from getting in the top. These are great for snorkeling in rough water.

Wet suits

In all but the warmest water, a wet suit makes snorkeling more comfortable. It can also protect you from jellyfish stings.

Special design at top prevents water from coming in

Clip attaches snorkel to mask

Flexible section adds comfort

Mouthpiece

Purge valve helps water escape

A typical modern snorkel.

Wet suits are made of neoprene, a soft, stretchy material.

Where to snorkel

Snorkeling is not much fun in deep or murky water, or water with nothing in it to see. The best places to snorkel have clear water and a variety of sea life.

Taking a snorkeling course with your friends is a good way to find out if you enjoy snorkeling.

Learning to snorkel

A swimming pool is the safest place to learn to snorkel. An instructor can help you master the basic skills, and will be there to help if anything goes wrong.

Diving clubs can also help you learn to snorkel. You can get in contact with them through your local swimming pool or dive shop.

Reef snorkeling

Coral reefs are very popular places for snorkeling. These are shallow areas where tiny sea creatures have built amazing, complicated shapes, called coral. Fish and other animals live in the coral, so there is always plenty to see.

Shipwrecks

Some shipwrecks lie in shallow water. They act like a mini-reef, providing shelter for fish and other sea life. Floating near a wreck can be a great way to watch underwater life.

Places to avoid

There are some places where snorkeling is not a very good idea:

- areas that are busy with jet skis, waterskiing, and other boating activity
- anywhere with strong **tides** or fast-flowing **currents**
- areas where there are alligators or other dangerous sea life

Coral reefs are popular for snorkeling because they are so rich in sea life.

WATCH OUT!

Never swim inside a shipwreck or cave. If you get trapped, you risk drowning.

Getting into the water

The first thing you have to do when snorkeling is get into the water. There are different techniques depending on whether you are getting in from a beach, boat, or jetty.

From the beach

Getting into the water from the beach can be tricky, especially if there are waves. The best way is to put on your mask, snorkel, and fins at the edge of the water. Turn around to face the beach, and walk backward into the water. This way, your fins will not make it hard to walk. As soon as the water is deep enough, turn around and swim out.

In rougher water, walking out backward with your fins on is a useful technique.

From a boat or jetty

If you are getting in from a boat or jetty, check the depth of the water. If you are unsure how deep the water is, gently lower yourself in. If you are sure the water is deep enough, you could try a divers' technique called the giant stride.

WATCH OUT!

Make sure the water is deep enough for a giant stride. At least shoulder-deep is best.

Technique

The giant stride

The giant stride is a good way to get into deeper water from a boat or jetty.

1 Stand on the edge of a secure platform, with about half your fins sticking out over the water.

2 Check that the water is clear of other snorkelers or anything you could land on.

3 Have your snorkel in your mouth. Use your hand to hold your mask securely on your face.

4 Look straight out at the **horizon** and take a big, smooth step forward. If you look down at the water, you will probably go in face-first!

Saving Energy

Whenever you are in the water, it is a good idea to use the smallest amount of energy possible. This will mean you can snorkel farther and stay in the water longer.

A streamlined shape

A streamlined shape is one that allows you to glide through the water as easily as possible. If your shape is not streamlined, your body will create **resistance** and **drag**. This means that you will need to use extra energy to push yourself through the water.

1 The straight line body shape is a good, streamlined shape. The water flows easily past the snorkeler.

2 Holding the body bent upward creates resistance at the snorkeler's chest and drag at their back. Both of these will slow the snorkeler down.

3 Swimming bent downward creates resistance at the snorkeler's back and drag at their chest.

Using your fins

Using your fins **efficiently** is a good way to save energy while in the water. Once you have learned to kick well, it will be easy to swim using only the movements of your legs. Your hands can dangle by your sides as you swim along.

Technique

The flutter kick

This describes the flutter kick, which snorkelers and divers use most of the time. Your fins flutter behind you with a constant gentle movement through the water.

1 Float in the water with your legs relaxed.
2 Make small kicks, first with one leg, then the other. Point your toes and kick using your hips and knees equally. Be careful not to use your knees too much. Keep your ankles relaxed.
3 Keep your fins below the surface. If they flap up into the air it wastes energy, and the noise scares fish away.
4 Keep your kicks even and smooth.

Top tip!

Small, smooth kicks are much better than big ones.

Clearing your snorkel and mask

Some snorkels fill with water every time you dive below the surface. Masks can also get water inside them. Fortunately, it is easy to clear the water out again.

Clearing your snorkel

Many snorkels are specially designed to keep water from getting into them. Others fill with water every time you dive. If you are using one of these, it is very easy to clear the water out. Once you are back at the surface, give a good puff of breath through the snorkel. All the water should shoot out the top, like when a whale comes to the surface.

 Top tip!

Practice clearing water out of your mask and snorkel in a pool. Then you will be confident if you have to do it in the sea.

It is important to know how to clear your snorkel before you dive.

Clearing your mask

Clearing your mask takes about 10 seconds. It can be done with your face underwater once you have practiced the technique. You need to be able to breathe in through your snorkel while clearing your mask.

Top tip!

If your mask is leaky, check for twisted straps, a cracked seal, or hair inside the seal.

Technique

Clearing your mask underwater

This is how to clear your mask underwater.

1 Gently tilt your head backward.

2 Use your hand to press the top of your mask against your forehead.

3 Take a breath through your snorkel. Breathe it out gently into the mask, through your nose.

4 When the mask is clear of water, stop pushing on it. You are ready for more underwater sightseeing.

Snorkeling safely

Snorkeling is a simple activity, but it takes place in a dangerous environment—underwater. These safety guidelines will help make your snorkeling safer.

Never put your hand or arm into a hole underwater, in case it gets stuck.

What can go wrong?

The three main dangers for snorkelers are:

- getting too tired to swim to safety
- getting dangerously cold
- becoming trapped underwater

Always make sure you have plenty of energy left. If you leave the water feeling tired, you have stayed in for too long. Always wear a wet suit if the water is less than body temperature—if it feels cold when you get in. And never get into a situation where you could be trapped underwater.

Top tip!

In an emergency, try to stay calm. Signal for help by waving one or both arms above your head. This is an international signal for "Help!"

The buddy system in action. Each snorkeler is looking out for the other.

The buddy system

Always snorkel with a partner, or buddy. Keep an eye on each other. If one of you gets into difficulty, the other can help, or raise the alarm.

Know your limits

Ask yourself some questions as a way of deciding the limits of safety for a snorkeling session.

How far can I swim?

Remember that you will be diving down as well as swimming along, so you may end up swimming farther than you think. You also have to get back to shore or to the boat. Make sure you have enough energy left.

How rough is the water?

Rough water is difficult to snorkel and swim in, so be extra-cautious if there are any choppy waves.

How fit is my buddy?

Never push your buddy to keep up. One of you could be a less experienced snorkeler or swimmer. That person is the one who sets the limits of safety.

"[Water occupies] about two-thirds of a world made for man— who has no gills."

Ambrose Bierce, U.S. writer, with a reminder that humans are not built for life without air.

Scuba diving

Scuba divers carry tanks strapped to their backs. The tanks contain air, which the diver breathes through a special device called a regulator. Regulators allow divers to take the right amount of air from their tanks with each breath.

Advantages of scuba diving

The biggest advantage of scuba diving is that you can stay underwater for much longer than if you were snorkeling. Most snorkelers can only stay below the surface for about 30 seconds. Divers can sometimes stay underwater for over an hour.

Scuba divers are also able to dive much deeper than snorkelers. They can reach depths of 115 feet (35 m) or more, where most snorkelers only go down about 16 feet (5 m). This makes scuba diving great for exploring deeper into the ocean.

Many shipwrecks have been discovered and explored by scuba divers.

Disadvantages of scuba diving

Scuba diving has several disadvantages when compared to snorkeling.

- The equipment costs thousands of dollars, even if it is second hand. It has to be checked by an expert regularly, which costs more money.
- The equipment is heavy and big, so it is hard to lug around without a car.
- More people die in scuba diving accidents than in snorkeling.

The biggest disadvantage is that in most countries you have to be at least 12 years old to train for scuba diving.

"You know as well as I do, Professor, that man can live underwater, providing he carries a sufficient supply of breathable air."

Captain Nemo in 20,000 Leagues Under the Sea by Jules Verne.

Scuba diving equipment is heavy and can be hard to carry around.

Underwater science

Understanding some of the science of snorkeling and diving will help make your time in the water safer and more fun.

Buoyancy

Buoyancy describes how well things float. People are more buoyant than water. This means that they naturally float to the surface. This is great for snorkeling, but not so good for divers. Divers wear a weight belt, which helps them stay near the seabed instead of floating back to the surface as soon as they swim down.

When divers want to come back to the surface, they use air from their tank to fill a buoyancy compensator. The buoyancy compensator helps them back up to the surface, like a hot-air balloon attached to their chest.

"I wanted to be an Olympic swimmer, but I had some problems with buoyancy."
Woody Allen. U.S. filmmaker.

Divers use a buoyancy compensator vest with air in it to help them come up to the surface slowly.

Pressure

Pressure underwater is the weight of water pressing down on your body. As you swim down deeper, the pressure gets greater. This is because there is more water above you, pressing down. At great depths, the pressure can crush and twist even metal submarines. Fortunately, snorkelers and divers never go that deep.

Technique

Clearing your ears

Underwater pressure affects people's ears, and they can start to hurt as you swim deeper. Use this technique to keep your ears clear of pain.

1 Pinch your nose lightly.

2 Either swallow or blow gently against your nose.

3 The pressure should clear.

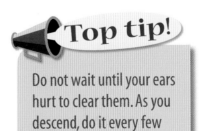

Do not wait until your ears hurt to clear them. As you descend, do it every few feet, before they start to hurt.

On shallow reefs like this one in the Red Sea snorkelers and divers can enjoy all the colors of the rainbow.

Underwater changes

The underwater world is very different from the world above the surface. Colors, sound, and temperature are all affected by being underwater.

Seeing

The water changes the way people see things. Objects look about 25 percent closer than they really are. They also look about 33 percent bigger. As you dive deeper, colors begin to disappear. At 33 feet (10 m), reds, oranges, and yellows are no longer visible. At 66 feet (20 m), greens disappear, too. After about 115 feet (35 m), even the blues disappear, and only gray is left.

Temperature

Deeper water is usually colder than the water at the surface. This is because surface water is warmed by the sun's rays. The sun's heat does not penetrate far below the surface.

Only blue-colored light penetrates below about 66 feet (20 m) of water. This is why deep sea often looks blue.

Hearing

People hear differently underwater. Sound travels very quickly—four times as fast as through air. While the noise of a parrot fish biting chunks off a coral reef will travel clearly, it might not be easy to figure out which direction the noise is coming from.

Cold and hypothermia

Body heat is lost much more quickly through water than through air that is the same temperature. Unless the water is at least as warm as your body temperature (99 °F), you risk getting **hypothermia**. This is very dangerous. In extreme cases, hypothermia can kill.

WATCH OUT!

The warning signs for hypothermia include:
- shivering
- numbness
- blurry or lost vision
- feeling sleepy, dizzy, or confused

These divers will definitely need their wet suits to help them keep warm. But even in warmer water, a wet suit is often needed.

Fit for the ocean

Snorkeling and diving are open to most people. You do not need to be a highly trained fitness fanatic to enjoy being underwater. Even so, a basic level of fitness is important.

Swimming

Swimming training is useful in two ways:

- Swimming helps you get fit for the same kind of activity you will be doing while diving or snorkeling. Swimming is especially good for your **lungs**, which will help your breath last longer while you are underwater.
- Swimming helps you get used to being in the water. This helps you stay calm underwater, which is especially useful for divers. Divers who are anxious breathe more deeply and use up their air faster than calm divers.

Some snorkelers find that swimming training helps make their lungs stronger, so that they can make a breath last longer underwater.

Diving requirements

In most countries, you must pass some physical tests to begin training as a diver. These include a test to make sure that your lungs are strong enough. There is also a swimming test. Normally, at the start of a training course, you have to be able to swim about 650 feet (198 m) without stopping, and about 26 feet (8 m) underwater without a push-off. By the end of the course, this will have increased to 980 feet (299 m) and 50 feet (15 m).

Who cannot dive?

Very few people cannot dive. Even people with asthma, diabetes, or physical disabilities may be able to train as divers, but they need to check with their doctor first. People who suffer from epilepsy cannot go diving.

"All you have to be is comfortable in the water. You need to be in good health, especially your ears. Given that, anybody can free-dive."

Tanya Streeter, world free-diving champion.

These divers are practicing sharing air from the same tank, in case one of them runs out of air.

Snorkeling and diving around the world

The most popular snorkel and dive sites in the world are usually either reefs or shipwrecks. These are just a few.

Warships and submarines

Name Scapa Flow

Location Orkney Islands, UK

Description Almost 100 warships, including two German submarines, lie at the bottom of the natural harbor at Scapa Flow.

Dive sites in the Red Sea

Name Marsa Alam

Location Red Sea, Egypt

Description Several dive sites can be reached from Marsa Alam. Some are miles out in the Red Sea, others a few hundred feet from the beach.

Underwater canyons and coral reefs

Name Pemba Island

Location Indian Ocean, Tanzania

Description An underwater canyon separates Pemba Island from the African mainland. Diving along the canyon and on the coral reefs is an unforgettable experience.

Shipwreck!

Name Tulamben

Location Bali Sea, Bali, Indonesia

Description Divers flock to see the wreck of the USS Liberty and the sea life that now lives there. Night-time divers sometimes spot lantern fish here.

Best in North America

Name   Dry Tortugas National Park
Location   Florida, United States
Description   Some of the best snorkeling in North America, with a shallow reef and the wreck of the *Windjammer* to explore.

Magical reef

Name   Madang
Location   Papua New Guinea
Description   Reef and wreck diving, including the chance to dive with **manta rays** at a site known as the Magic Passage.

Clear Caribbean waters

Name   Bonaire
Location   Bonaire, Caribbean Sea
Description   Bonaire is a tiny island with over 80 diving sites and amazingly clear water. Great for divers and snorkelers, because many good places are just off the beach.

Reefs and wrecks

Name   Great Barrier Reef
Location   Pacific Ocean, Australia
Description   Actually a line of almost 3,000 reefs, there is something here for everyone, snorkelers and divers alike, including shallow coral, steep walls, and wrecks.

Interview: Underwater crazy!

Rowena first started snorkeling when she was seven years old, while on vacation with her parents. She now works as a diving instructor.

What is it you like about being underwater?
I like the peace of just being able to float in this beautiful world. The fish, coral, and other living things make me feel really close to nature, even though underwater is an alien environment for humans!

Which do you prefer—snorkeling or diving?
Hmm. Well, diving's great because you get to stay underwater for a long time. But there is a lot of equipment in diving. Sometimes I love the simplicity of snorkeling, especially in shallow water where all the action is close to the surface.

What is your favorite place for snorkeling and diving?
The Great Barrier Reef in Australia is great for both. I really liked snorkeling in Bali, and the diving in the Caribbean is fantastic.

What would you be if you were not a diver?
I can't imagine that! I love the ocean so much I think it would have to be something to do with the sea—an **oceanographer**?

And finally, what is your favorite diving book?
That has to be *Diving Australia* by Neville Coleman and Nigel Marsh! It's a fantastic guide to some of the best underwater spots in Australia. It makes me want to go traveling whenever I pick it up!

Glossary

currents
strong flows of water in a particular direction

drag
a pull backward on a moving object

efficiently
with the minimum amount of effort, to save energy

horizon
the line where the land meets the sky

hypothermia
dangerously low body temperature, which can cause the heart to stop beating properly

lungs
the part of our body we use to breathe

manta rays
large, flat fish that skim through the water by moving their wings

oceanographer
a scientist who studies the oceans, how they work, and the life they contain

resistance
a push against something

tides
the rise and fall of the sea, which happens roughly once every 12 hours

Index

A

air tanks 7, 20, 22

B

benefits of sport 4
buddy system 5, 19
buoyancy 22
buoyancy compensator 22

C

caves 11
clearing ears 23
clearing mask 17
clearing snorkel 16
coral reefs 11, 25, 28, 29
cost 6, 21
currents 11

D

diving clubs 10
diving depths 20, 23, 24
diving instructor 10, 30
drag 14

E

energy efficiency 14–15
exercise 4, 26

F

fins 5, 8, 12, 13, 15
fitness 26–27
flutter kick 15

G

giant stride 13

H

hearing underwater 25
hypothermia 25

L

learning to snorkel 10
lungs 26

M

mask 5, 8, 12, 13, 16, 17
mouthpiece 9

P

purge valve 9

R

regulator 20
resistance 14

S

safety 18–19
scuba diving 20–21
shipwrecks 11, 20, 28, 29
snorkel 5, 6, 9, 12, 13, 16, 17
snorkel and dive sites 28–9
streamlined shape 14
swimming 14, 15, 26, 27

T

temperature 18, 24
tides 11

U

underwater dangers 11, 18, 25

V

vision underwater 24

W

water pressure 23
weight belt 22
wet suit 5, 8, 9, 18, 25